POEMS FOR THE OLDER CROWD:

The Terminally Mature

JAMES LITTLE

DORRANCE
PUBLISHING CO
EST. 1920
PITTSBURGH, PENNSYLVANIA 15238

Dorrance Publishing Co
585 Alpha Drive
Pittsburgh, PA 15238
Visit our website at *www.dorrancebookstore.com*

ISBN: 978-1-6393-7033-7
eISBN: 978-1-6393-7822-7

POEMS FOR THE OLDER CROWD:

The Terminally Mature

Introduction:

I am a young old person. Hopefully I will become a mature old person. Muscles and joints ache. My endurance is failing. I avoid things that used to be easy.

I thought that maybe there are others who have similar problems. I wanted to speak to them and share some of my anxieties.

I don't want to be depressive, just honest. I hope we can join together and become strong by being united. We need to stand and assert ourselves. We are not done. We have much to give. We have earned the right to be taken seriously. The superficiality of age should not bring shame. We will not be ignored. We will not recede. We will go down with all flags flying!

"James"

My personality
Is like a cloudy summer's day.
You sense the warmth
And acknowledge
There is a sun shining brightly
 behind all those mysterious layers.

But the fog is so thick
That only faint glimpses
of the possibilities
make their muted impressions
on your soul.

You content yourself
 with knowing
that a positive presence is near
if only the clouds would part
and reveal
The sunshine held within.

And when the light rays
Do penetrate
It makes you wish
and wonder
why could it not always be so.

"Admiration"

I love the old gnarled things,
Images twisted and bent.
Objects with dents and dings,
Resurrected, heaven sent.

Mankind glowing with age.
Wisdom encased to their cores.
Courage to turn each page,
Security only bores.

Patinas exquisite,
Seasoned through experience.
Intentions implicit,
Exuding deference.

Aged roots running deep,
Scarred from personal trials.
Lifelong secrets they Keep
Content in their denials.

Ambitions not yet spent
Enliven their survival.
Compassion their intent,
Surpassing younger rivals.

All have mastered by heart
Their life's historical play.
Each award-winning part
Earned for living their own way.

"Rest Home Blues"

A life composed of only memories, how sad.
Never looking forward only to what you had.
Today at the "Home" elders receive physical care.
But often their emotions are laid bare.

Our elders' world has been shrinking.
From farm to townhouse I am thinking.
From house to apartment to assisted living.
Next, to a nursing home, no quarter giving.

Living space has shrunk from acres to a lot.
Next, two rooms, then one room, spacious it is not.
Then no rooms, only a cemetery plot.
Shoulder to shoulder in their appointed slot.

They descended from world travel on airplanes
To car trips around our country on four lanes.
The descent continues to bus excursions
And then around the area, one-day diversions.

Over to the city for a shopping trip.
Then downtown for mail. Best sure not to slip.
Next just outside to get some fresh air.
Then best stay inside, an air-conditioned lair.

Old Age? A balloon forgotten behind the couch
Slowly silently deflating. Ouch!
One hopes the Knot was tightly tied.
Perhaps such feelings are best Kept inside.

"A Fool's Scheme"

Just an old man with nothing to do,
Bored with the old, afraid of the new.
A drooping man who is no longer cool.
A determined man not yet a fool.
A gentle man who has lost his anger.
A small-town man but not a wrangler,
An earnest man who just does not fit.
A man who would rather work than sit.
A dreamer not totally awake.
Not quite ready his life to forsake.
Silently looking for his fast dance,
To ante up and take a chance.
Trying to enumerate his worth.
Concerning his end, he sees no mirth.
Trying to accomplish one last thing
Before the bells for him do ring.

"Cautious Neurotic"

Excess happiness causes bad luck.
Be wary or in trouble you're stuck.
Be very careful in whatever you do,
All that you do will be done to you.
Too much confidence will bring you down.
Too many smiles will cause you to frown.
Don't invite disaster, be on guard.
Celebrating should always be hard.
Don't make mistakes; They will be your doom.
Spontaneity will end in gloom.
Bright optimism brings down a curse,
Don't worry, it will always get worse.
Control your world or all will crumble.
Don't forget to always be humble.
Never deviate, don't take a chance.
Doing the obvious is the best stance.
To every whim you must not cater.
Catastrophe, sooner or later.
Assume the worst, always double check.
Give up now, what the heck?

"Beginning to Fade"

There was a time when I was fearless.
I was younger then, I must confess.
My plans and goals did not seem immense.
I had no thought of the consequence.

Now problems and flaws are all I see.
The stresses of life I seek to flee.
Is this ancient wisdom in my head
Or neurotic thoughts which must be fed?
Overly cautious I've come to be.

My physical prowess seems to fade
As years of toil at my feet are laid.
Is a tottering elder my fate?
Who survives longer, me or my mate?
If need be, who would come to our aid?

Scrimping and saving done with planning
To regain control, constant scanning.
Weaving our way through uncertain life,
Wishing for luck through all our strife.
A fortress of hope we are manning.

Why Pessimism?

The furnace isn't working properly.
The sewer backs up intermittently.
The shingles wear out prematurely.
The car needs repair constantly.
The faucet drips continually.
The fuses blow unexpectedly.
The lawn needs mowing aggressively.
The paint peels unassumingly.
The water seeps aggravatingly.
The roof leaks irritatingly.
The wife ignored unabashedly.
The money declines inconspicuously.
The waistline increases insidiously.
My stamina decreases abhorrently.
My drinkage changes imperceptibly.
Old age looms ominously.

"I am Me"

I was born of lowly birth,
No silver spoon to prove my worth.
I grew up with stone and wood,
Sweat on my brow was understood.
The earth's sweet stench between my toes,
No Wall Street bliss to cure my woes.
To do or die was all I knew,
The upper crust was reserved for few.
Handwritten letters in the postal mail,
Stilted conversations without fail.
Still, we managed to survive.
We got a hand up.
We just wanted to stay alive
To drink from Time's cup.
We've earned an old age with dignity.
We don't need politician's superficiality.
Let us die as we are livin',
Proud of the niche that God has given.
We have earned our place in our lifetime plot,
We ask for no more, thanks a lot.

"Sunset Premonition"

This would be the death I was meant to die,
Drinking champagne and watching the sky.
When my end days come and I have no worth,
Celebrate the occasion as if a birth.
For this is the day I've been waiting for,
A hallelujah chorus could not ask for more.
My trials are done, my sins are forgiven,
This is the time for which I have been living.
So raise a toast,
Who can shout the most?
Praise the man who is leaving.
Laughter is what I want to hear
Instead of grieving!

"Neurotic"

The simple truth of the matter,
We are born,
We live,
We die.
Nothing can change that.
Some say the young never think of death.
Not me!
It was constantly on my mind;
    The fear of falling, crashing
    Drowning, suffocating, bleeding.
In later life add heart attack,
    Stroke, cancer, organ failure.
Oh! The things I did not do to avoid death.
Now most of my life is over.
All I want to do
Is wait safely in my house
And hope for an easy end.

Will it come at home
Or in a hospital?
Perhaps a nursing home
Sometimes I wonder
If I ever really lived?
I wonder what it would be like now
If I had taken chances?

"The Best Way"

I get into ruts.
I mean, I like routine.
I look for the most efficient way.
Then I repeat that procedure
Exactly the same way
Each time I do it.
I can't help it.
It just seems right,
I always want to do things
The right way.
I like knowing
What's going to happen next.
No surprises,
Ruts are comforting.
Ruts are safe.
Being safe
Is the most important thing.
I like ruts.

"Dusk"

It's nice when the light fades.
All the errors and defects
Begin to mellow
Making me a contented fellow.
Forms and shadows
Begin to blend.
Nothing is exactly what it was.
Better by far
Without the scar
Of reality.
The mood is soft.
The hubbub settles,
Perfection seems possible.
Almost time for candle glow,
This I know,
The encroaching night
Seems as a friend
Eager to listen and praise you
For what you are,
Not for what you have been
Or could be in the end.

"My Reality"

I don't understand the young.
That part of me is done.
Enough said.

Unless, it is toddlers
Salivating over chocolate chips.
Or a newborn
Clinging to my fingertips.
Or a preschooler
Ripping open Christmas gifts.

Perhaps it is just teenagers
I resent.
Unless they are taking a driver's test
In a car that was lent.
Or faking a grade report
To avoid an angry retort.
Or driving to a first date,
Better early than late.

Yes, I have no time
For the young.
Mainly, since they have no time for me.
You see,
I still remember how it was
And will never be again.

"Untitled #68"

There was a man,
Long ago
Who owned a piece of wood.
He gazed at it lovingly
As days passed by.
It was unique.
It had potential
Or so it seemed.
He spoke to his friends about it
And all agreed.
Something should be done.
But no one had the time
Or money.
So it set quietly,
Unassumedly,
Just lolling in the sun
And the rain
And the snow
And the frost
Until it began to fade
And rot.
Just a little at first
Then all agreed it was past its prime.
Nothing to be done.
So it was cast into a campfire
For all the family to enjoy,
A few sparks and that was it.

"On Having Loved"

What is it that connects people?
I know you will say it is love.
But what is love?
I do not understand.
Is it when you take out the garbage
When it is not your turn?
Is it when you make conversation
When you would rather watch TV?
Is it when you say it is great
When it is just okay?
Is it when you wonder
How you could ever survive
If she were not around?
Is it not being able to talk
Because there are no words?
All this and more
But more than that.
It is Knowing that we can never be separated
No matter what our fate.
Life and death
A mere day and night.
No fright.
Our souls unite
Eternally.

"Memories"

Memories are collectibles,
To time they are susceptible.
A fondness for a younger day,
Sentimentality holding sway.
Fragile images lead astray.
Anger and anxiety fade away.
Polished, waiting on display,
Cherished in a special way
They strike a spark and ignite
Soulful feelings from the past
That arouse but cannot last,
Faint flickers on sudden flights.
They are sheltered in love to preserve
Small bits of joy from life's reserve.
Antiques engraved upon our face
Proudly worn with modest grace.
Simple rewards that we embrace
For dwelling in the human race.

"For Sale"

Who is this old geezer
Carrying me around?
A certified wheezer,
Can no better transportation be found?

I prefer a younger model
With spritely step,
No need to coddle,
Full of pep.

This abode, chilly in winter,
Summer's heat does offend.
If wooden blocks he does splinter
This body takes a week to mend.

A habitual frowning face,
A sight quite depressing,
Of early joyous times shows no trace
An attitude that needs redressing.

A decrepit, old harmless codger,
Unworthy of my exalted status.
This weak-kneed future rest-home lodger
Definitely now a person non-gratis.

"Recycling"

Parents revive their youth through their children
When these lives diminish
They relive again with grandchildren
Until they reach their finish.

But if there is time
For one more round
A great-grandchild
Brings joy profound.

They spend a lifetime
With overflowing cup,
Always concerned
With growing up.

So it has been
Since time has begun,
Worn out bodies
Remaining young.

Yet, the barren few
Cannot renew
By simply starting over,

They must face
The mild disgrace
That they are getting older

"Obituary"

I was just reading the morning news.
An old friend passed yesterday.
I was grocery shopping,
Trying to pick up a few things.
A few blocks away
Cars were gathered at a house.
Family had arrived
It was plain to see
As their neighbor
Finished mowing his lawn.
Relatives had made fresh coffee
As I trudged to the bank
Before my deposit was late.
And then silence,
An old one had breathed their last,
Decades of pain and pleasure
From times long past.
Church services galore.
But I had to go to the hardware store
For some garbage bags
Calls were made.
Tears were shed.
I had to get supper on.
My spouse would be home soon
With expectations.

"Downsizing"

Why do I feel so antsy
In my latter years?
What's the hurry?
Why the fears?
No need to scurry
Into a safer rat hole.
As if being efficient
Would soothe my soul
And delay the inevitable.
What's the need to tidy up,
Eliminate excesses
And become so pristine?
I've labored with this junk
All my life.
Such advice is total bunk.
Now it's their turn to inherit
And learn to bear it,
Pretending it makes them richer.
Or do they prefer cash instead of trash?
Why should I care?
It's their problem;
I'm outta here!

"End of Day"

I remember this time from my youth,
Gazing into the distance
Across highway 52.
To experience it once more
Floods the memory.
The sun is receding,
 The temperature moderates,
Seems cool almost.
The traffic softens.
Someone is mowing in the distance.
Vibrations flood the senses,
Almost sexual,
A special time
Between now and then.
Muffled voices drift
From across the street.
Birds are giving it their last hurrah,
Anticipating the mourning Dove.
It's haunting refrain
Triggers my melancholy.
The quiet time,
The dying time
Is upon us.

"Secular Supplication"

Oft times when the sun is sinking
And I seek the cradles rest
My ego ceases thinking
My mind is blank at best.
The sounds of the ambitious
Soften with time.
I need solitude's serenity
As I search for the rhyme
To justify ego-centricity,
A phrase that I can present
At judgement
To justify the strife
And silliness
Of my wasted life.
Words that would open
To the least position in heaven
Is all I am praying for
Tomorrow as the sun is rising
I begin my task again
Of justifying my existence,
A game I cannot win.

"Village Kids"

Just off old highway 52 heading west
Snaked a dusty narrow gravel lane
Which forked and passed a quarry pit
Then descended sharply into a narrow valley,
Treetops on each side of the path
Intertwining
Shady and cool
The road meandered past a tiny, chilling cave
With clear cold spring water gurgling,
Drinkable.
At the hill's bottom stood
A small concrete bridge
With wading pool
Frequently dammed
With errant mossy limestone rocks,
A fish or two though no one cared.
It's where we rode our ponies
Bareback
And whacked brothers with cattails,
Waded knee deep searching for fossils,
Lit timid little campfires,
Wrote signals in the air
Swirling charred smoking sticks.
Just on sultry days
When there was nothing to do.
No one seemed to care
That we were Trespassing.

"The Old Man on the Corner"

He will not accept your contempt
Nor does he seek your approval.
He lives the solitary life.
No chit chat.
No bacon fat.
No simpering fools.
No lustful drools.
A hard, straight line
No noose of dread
Poised above his head.
Alone,
But never by himself.
Myriad teeming fantasies
Stacked upon his shelf.
Unlock that door,
Out they pour.
Hang them on the wall.
Seductive fiends
At his beck and call.

"The End's Beginning"

That is the way it goes.
Someone unloads their stash.
Since you have the cash
It is yours.
A lifetime of collecting
Gone in a flash.
The need was great
Or so it seemed.
Who could have dreamed
They would be so lucky
To inherit another's passion.
 And so it flows in unending fashion
From person to person.
What was yours
Is now mine.
And when my time comes
I hope to be so lucky
As to encounter one
Willing to siphon my fun
And allow me to rest
With memories of my best.
I wonder if the time will come
When this sequence is ever done.
I will take that bet,
It has not happened yet.

"All I Can Afford"

I went to the lesser part of town today,
The part that's a little slumpy,
A little dumpy,
The great grandfathers of the housing family.
The ones that are a little raggedy,
A little jaggedy, a little saggedy.
The ones that have endured
A hundred-plus subzero winters
Whose splinters
Are encased in aluminum
Whose plumbing patched in plastic
Still serves God's people
Through winter's chill or summer magic.
Whose children still catch the bus
Or walk to school without fuss
Where daughters' girlfriends still gather
For after-hour escapades.
Mothers' lovers still pull the shades on Friday nights
Babysitting clients stop for coffee
Or maybe a beer, a little cheer
Before boyfriends gently rap
And mumble to mothers
They'll be back by twelve.
How many generations of life
Before the house gets the knife
And is hauled away
Progress,
More or less.

"Nurses"

The old may seem pathetic,
Physically arthritic
But they are simply waiting,
Anticipating the appointed time
Of transportation.
They have passed their test,
Punched their ticket
And now take their rest
Awaiting emancipation.
Memories of a fuzzy past
Should not last,
Slowly becoming numb,
Practice for a new life to come.
Their seat is assured, waiting for passage
To their eternal abode.
We nurses maintain their bodies,
Uplift their spirits
Until their vehicle
Makes its appearance.
We wish them a safe trip
Knowing that finally
Everything will be okay

"Sundays With Dad"

I approach our church
Somewhat apprehensive,
Trying not to be defensive
As I find my pew
Where I sit
As I always do.
Things go smoothly
Until the hymn has begun
The ones my father always had sung
Around the house
Early Sunday mornings
As he prepared for worship.
I stare at the stained glass
So no one will detect
My glistening eyes.
I cannot speak
As my composure I seek.
His memory overwhelms.
Still, I follow the words
Haltingly in my mind
Embarrassing,
To cry in church.
So I slip my finger to my eye
And wipe away the tears. Will it be long?
How many years
Before I can sing his song?

"For Men Only"

I want to be a curmudgeon
Don't want to shave,
Don't want to comb my hair
Don't want to behave.
I want to walk the streets
In the middle of the night
If I am grody
Don't want to keep out of sight
The latest fashion
Doesn't interest me.
Rubber boots and overalls
Are as good as it needs to be

I want to be a curmudgeon
Not interested in your views.
Rather have a drink
Than watch the evening news
Not such a bad guy
I think you'll see.
Really just don't care
What you think of me.
Don't want to play your game.
Don't want to be the same
I'll still take a bath
To avoid my good wife's wrath.

"Obits"

I am always curious about their ages.
How many years did they endure?
Trying to ferret out people
Whom I have beaten.
The last sad competition of humanity,
Feeling superior to the dead.

"Stage Three"
Waiting to die
Is like sitting outside
The music instructor's office
Waiting for a lesson
For which you did not practice.

"End Stage"

Final Preparation.
Ambiguous Deadline.
Smooth Transition.

    Cool.
    Calm.
    Silent.
Prearranged Responsibilities.
No Ostentation.
Automatic Execution.

    No Muss.
    No Fuss.
    No Problem.
The End
Or
The Beginning.

"Prognosis"

It is a shock
When it happens.
We prefer
To live in denial.
I was informed
My systems are failing.
I have entered a new phase,
Old Age.
He is my constant companion.
A subtle reminder,
Time is short,
Live Well.

"Just the Facts"

Ideas?
Oh yes,
I had ideas!
I was thought to be
Very creative!
Unfortunately,
None of those ideas
Amounted to much.
My good marriage
Saved me.
Made me a little bit
Respectable.
Just a bit.
I have accepted my fate.
A quiet loser
With a perky wife.

"The Golden Years"

No longer
Boundless energy
For overcoming
Foolish mistakes,
Cautious wisdom.
Meticulous planning.
Bobbing and weaving
Through fleeting days
Hoping the money will last.
Expecting a modicum
Of respect
And tiny morsels
Of patience
From loved ones.
Resigned to the inevitable.
Anticipating the prize.

"Perspective"

25
Time meant forever.
45
It was not too late.
60
It would not happen.
70
What would I do?
Now I think in days,
Not years.
Every day is an opportunity
To be productive,
To be helpful,
To be understanding,
To be kind,
To be forgiving,
To be gentle.
So when it is just a matter of hours
I can say it was all worthwhile.

"Change"

To the women
Who are left alone
Against their will
With little mercy shone,
I wish you the courage
Until the pain relents.
Such courage is truly heaven sent.
Change is the curse
Of the survivors.
For better or worse
A new life is yours,
Patience is a must.
Be gentle
Be just.
Take your rest
And Know
You have loved the best.

"Premonition"

My quiet friend
Paid me a visit again.
Uninvited, he kept to the shadows,
An unearthly presence
Nestled in the corner.
I sensed his silent conversation
Coursing through my bones.
Not his final visit,
Just a social call,
Strong curiosity
About how my days were going.
A strange fellow, he.
Unwelcome to no avail.
My resistance stifled his insistence,
Denial my only recourse.
I bade him farewell,
I could not go today.

"Autumnal Angst"

Witchy vibrations embrace the air.
Warm breezes,
Yet malevolence stirs a fear.
Like a strange car
Parked down the block.
Shrouded figures
Gaze out dark windows
Silently observing,
Waiting for an opportune time
To enact their ignominious plot.
We ignore,
Hoping for only a felonious mirage.
Deep down we know
This to be intractable reality.
Our time has come.
We chip out
Bits of happiness,
Stifle our anxiety
And wait for the inevitable.

"Sailing"

The Mainstay cracked today
And I, not knowing what to do,
Made a patch
And looked the other way.
I altered our course,
Steered for calmer waters
Where a crack might not matter.
Now moored at bay
We are pondering
How to sail over waves
That could send us to the bottom.
There were no storms
Just aged wood giving way.
Are we now to be a derelict
Resting in drydock?
Perhaps the patch will hold
And we can drift aimlessly
From port to port
Seeking nothing more
Than relaxation
And nothing less
Than satisfaction
Of a voyage well done.

"Little Valkyrie"

Come, little Valkyrie
Ride your wild one into the night
Heedless of danger
Mocking the fright.
Take the long journey
Away from the station.
Trek your last trip
To your final destination.
Laugh at the fear
When the end time is near.
Your fate has been sealed
Since the day of your birth
So fly, fly for all you are worth!

"Fragility"

Yes, I am dying.
I appear freakish
With sagging wrinkled flesh,
Veins blue and bulging,
Dark shadows encircling sunken eyes,
Hair, thin and wispy gray.
A multitude of tasks
I no longer attempt.
What happened to my Fortress?
Yet, deep inside my callow brain
A flame still brightly burns
As I feel myself
As a young vibrant youth
With all my silliness
And naïve desires still intact.
This is the person
Who will be missed,
Not this wretched body.
'though I love it's rickety ways.
It has served me well
And I will not despise it
Simply because of age.
My flesh fails
But my spirit will remain
Elevated
To the Astral Plane.

"New Realities"

Passing it down
From generation
As I was raised
Is now obsolete.
If it can't be sold
Throw it out in the street.
No one is interested
In your precious stuff.
A change in attitude
Is surely necessary
To avoid the pain
Of this latest rebuff.
Enjoy it while living
Right up to the end.
No generous giving
Will your memory extend.
Your life has been yours
That is enough.
When it is done
Don't burden the young.

"Persistence"

From time to time
A dark mood
Slices my psyche.
I play college tunes
Drifting back
To the sixties,
My time of success.
I wonder about Plan B or C.
Time is short,
Memory fades,
Little energy to care.
Yet, I do.
My tiny dream
Refuses to die.
Each time
When on life support
It revives
Begging me
To follow
Into the light.
Grudgingly, I trudge
After it
Wondering how much farther
To the end.
It ignores my complaining
Shouting,
IT NEVER ENDS!

"Musings"

I took the bait
And took a break
To do the essentials
I started late
But before my life is done
I have won a reprieve
To do what I believe.
Slow and steady
But I am ready
To empty my cup
Until each sup
Has been tasted.
Then I will know
As things do go
That my life
Was not wasted.

"Myrna"

It was the first time
I realized
Mother was frail.
Head bowed,
Chin on chest
Rising and falling
In the rhythm
Of slumber.
Thin wisps of hair
Atop dark creases
Of flesh.
She looked of death.
At least it seemed
The end was not far away.
No tears in my eyes
Just a lump in my throat
As my mind tried to remember
All the work
Those fingers had done for us.
No longer useful
Yet not a burden.
Our love could not save her.
If only I could make her happy
Once again.
At least for a day
On her ninety-ninth birthday
It was the best I could do.

So I wrote the check,
Placed it in a card
And hoped she would accept
My paltry effort.

"Normal, Like You"

I have always hated swimming.
I always sink.
I despise being wet.
I was born to be bone dry.
Now I am wading in reality
And yes,
I hate it.
But I am trying not to sink
And failing.
At my age
I should be content
To sit on the bottom,
No need to splash.
I could live down here
If I never knew
Others were bobbing
In the waves,
Sailing their boats,
Smug in their success.
I am destined
To be a bottom feeder
Trying to make a pearl
From a grain of sand.

"Enigma"

What to do
When the unknowable occurs,
The strange, unexpected,
Bizarre Thing,
The event with no
Plausible explanation
The happening that does not fit
With the physical laws
Of nature,
When the impossible
Becomes the possible?
Ignore the circumstances?
Pretend nonchalance?
Feign cautious naiveté?
Or for the spiritually inclined,
Celebrate unabashedly!
File it under "Supernatural,"
Accept we are not alone.
Just another trip
To the Mystic Zone.

"Quiet Times"

I am a solitary presence
In an empty room
Surrounded by my possessions
Sunday afternoon,
Silence
Except for the tranquil strains
Of classical melodies
Meandering through my door.
My thoughts drift back
To younger days
Surrounded by the intensity
Of an active life
With no thought
Of the tumult to come.
It is amazing
That I survived.
And now my only obstacle
Is how to amuse myself
In my remaining time.
This emptiness
Drags me down
And yet I am so fortunate
To have this problem.

Many fell silent
Along the way
I sit and wait patiently
For my conclusion
No sorrow,
Only acceptance.

"This Time"

When you accept death
Life becomes easier.
It is okay
To fade away.
No one
Would understand,
Not necessary
To hold my hand.
It has all been done.
The decisions were mine,
I was the one.
No one to blame,
The outcome
Would be the same.
I cannot
Avoid my fate.
So let's have a drink
And enjoy this time.
No need to think
Of past pains
Or lost loves.
Drain your glass
And rejoice
Let your voice
Fade into silence,
Your work is complete.
Believe.
You won!

"Bucolic Critics"

We live in a wine-stained house.
Big comfy chairs
Did not withstand the test of time.
No cat or dog hairs
Just chardonnay
And merlot
On display.
Remembrances
Of intimate conversations
With goose liver paté.
He preferred Robert Frost
And *Casablanca*.
She, *Pride and Prejudice*
But in wilder moments
Ricky Nelson and Paul Anka.
Champagne
With olive puffs
On special occasions.
No one was gruff
If purple passion
Flew through the air.
The exchange of opinions
Was why they were there.
Joe Cocker
Bouncing off stained glass,
A reluctant monastery
Of liberal agenda.

Brandy with vermouth
Enlivened Vincent Van Gogh.
Although a bit uncouth
Our lives were not a waste,
A mere reflection
Of artistic taste.

"Coach"

Ever try to make an old person
Lose fifty pounds?
Old people don't change their bodies,
They change their environment.
Lose weight
So they can navigate the bathtub?
Hell no!
Put in a different bathtub
Regardless of the cost
Or aesthetic devastation.
Extra weight
Hinders movement
So they move less,
Their muscles atrophy,
They become helpless,
Ride scooters in grocery stores,
Have clerks carry out their purchases,
Anything to avoid challenging themselves.
You have to fight
Against decrepitude.
It is a mental game
As much as physical
You won't like the "Home."
Stay in yours.
Meet the challenge.
Stay strong.
Stay independent.
EXERCISE!

"Obstinance"

The forecast warned:
Extremely Frigid.
Best stay indoors.
Hunker down
Until "Old Man Winter"
Regains his sanity.
We aged walkers
Utter our profanities
As we pile on layers
Of manmade warmth.
Best be prepared.
Arctic air
Has no mercy.
It does not care
About status or wealth
Or fragile health.
It will take you
To your final destination
If you should fall
Or invite pneumonia
Into your life.

We have survived
Decades of winter
And so despite the cost
We press our luck
And inflate our egos
By walking out the door
Just one more battle
With "Old Jack Frost."

"The Quiet Life"

I am a silent person,
I lead the quiet life.
Spent my days
In a small-town haze
Of trivialities.
No profound happenings
Intruded.
Contented myself
With family things,
Birthday parties
With a few friends,
Modest wedding
In the church.
Saved our money
For down payments
And such.
A healthy child
Did well in school,
Now off somewhere
On his own
With a pretty wife.
Retirement came,
More time for sewing
Or perhaps an art class.

Traveled out West
To see the mountains
And desert beauty.
Determined to die in my house
And save the money
Of a nursing home.
Visited my cemetery plot.
All is in order.

"Artistic Expression"

They say my art is weird,
Disturbing, unsettling, unnatural.
I say, "It definitely is not cute kittens
And puppies!"
It is an accurate reflection
Of my inner workings.
I could say,
"Three trips to the psych ward
Has warped my view of the world."
If truthful,
My mind has known pain
Since childhood.
No childhood trauma drama,
I was born a little twisted.
I knew fear from the beginning.
I have fine-tuned it over the years
And now it gushes out in lines, shapes
And colors.
The sight of pain personified
Upsets the insecure.
Now my walls abound
With paintings
Of my demented fiends
Stripped, defenseless, bare-naked
For the world to see.

Not so terrifying now,
Locked in their frames.
Still, my friends are speechless,
Unable to concoct a compliment.
Their silence is again painful
But at least I know
I put on a good show.

"Delinquent"

Are you sure
You want to do that
To me?
I am an island
In the middle
Of a raging sea.
I am a small,
Insignificant,
I barely thrive.
Yet, I have coconut palms,
Just enough to keep you alive
When you tire
Of fighting the waves
And success is just out of reach.
Crawl up my beach
For a place to sleep.
Light a fire.
Have something to eat
To give you strength
For another day of swimming.
Are you sure
You want to do that
To me?

"Intrepid Warrior"

I am fighting a battle
I cannot win.
Time will have its way.
My arrogance
Goads me on.
My false belief?
That determination
Will win the day.
The subtle
Downward slide
Ignored
By my desperate ego
Sucks me into an altered state
Of inflated pride
Denying bouts of vertigo.
Each day the battle rages
My resolve
Declines in stages.
Victory eludes me,
No truce will suffice.
This enemy is outrageous,
It refuses to make nice.
My inferiority is regrettable.
Despite all delaying tactics
The outcome is inevitable.
I reject such loss.
I take my rest.
Tomorrow I begin again.

"Stoic"

This year is my fiftieth year
Since I began my adult life.
Fifty years a failure
Is a heavy burden to bear.
It is enough to bring
Strong men to their knees.
I am not a strong man,
Yet here I stand
Refusing to bow my head.
Refusing to say "I'm sorry."
Each day I begin anew
Thinking perhaps this will be the time
It all comes together
And I can shed this shame.
Quitting is not an option
That resides in my core.
The flame burns low
But not out.
Silence has become my constant companion.
I have no words for the whiners.
Either you are strong enough to live
Or you die.
Nothing more to say.
Nothing to make it easy.

I have only a few more years
Or failure to endure.
When the end comes
I am quite sure
It will not be easy.

"Homecoming"

It takes awhile to get back to heaven.
The road may be rocky
With twists and turns
And uphill grades.
The path may darken
As memory fades.
The help of the merciful
Is sometimes needed
Exhausting our resources
As our sorrows and cares
Do not go unheeded.
It makes no difference
If we win this race
Since all the steep trials
End in the same place.
Have courage
As the years
And decades quickly pass.
Though your health slowly fades
And your steps do falter,
Don't be downhearted.
You are simply coming nearer
To the place where you started.

Role Model

I love the elderly,
The ones who are gentle and kind.
People who have mellowed
Exuding love and acceptance
To the humans they find.
They have left pettiness
And obstinance far behind.
For them
Each moment is memorable.
They are finally at peace
And have accepted their fate,
Making the most
Of the least,
Being grateful for each morsel
That comes their way.
Are there such people, you say?
I have known a few
At least one or two,
I was hoping to be one someday.

"Ordinary"

Some mornings
Before dawn
As I sit with my coffee cup
I struggle to remember
Happy memories from my past
And I must admit
There is little if anything
That I would do over.
The good things
Ended badly.
My goals
Were not met.
I do not weep for myself,
My life was sufficient.
The fantasy that at the end
I would overcome it all
And become a superstar
Will remain a myth.
No Hollywood ending for me.
I will recede gracefully
But I hold no misconceptions,
I failed.
But my spouse was a success
And I guess
My choice of mate
Propels me to the top.
Not so ordinary
After all.

Vietnam

My brother served.
Not a volunteer
But he went.
Became a Marine.
Honorable discharge.
Came home respected.
My number was not called.
Not the volunteering type.
I thought it was bogus.
A politician's war.
Of course,
I also did not want to die.
I played it safe.
Now, years later
Where is my honor?
Where is my pride?
A hollow life
Is what I created.
Yet, I avoided
The stench of death.
No midnight trauma
Invades my dreams.
Just a little shame
Around the edges
But not enough
To change my ways.

A coward's life
Is never mentioned
Only heroes
Share the limelight.
We did not get off easy.
Or did we?

"Old Friends"

We live in an antique house.
It is still quite sturdy
And all original
Though it could use a mascara touchup.
A trip to the beauty parlor
Would do it no harm.
It overflows with collectibles,
The result of our pack rat ardor.
A severe diet
Would put it on the mend.
That is not likely.
We inhabitants
Lack the stamina
For a makeover.
Since our bodies are slumping
We blend in quite well
With our archaic environment.
We are all jumping
To the same conclusion.
The burning question,
Which will collapse first
The owners
Or the real estate?
No need to go
To a holding cell
To await our fate.

Let's try to amuse ourselves
And enjoy the fellowship
Of our old friend.
We support each other
As best we can.

Family

I visit him
Once or twice a month
In the summer,
Especially in dry spells,
To water the geraniums
And pull weeds encroaching
Around the stones.
The red blossoms
Are striking
Against the mottled gray
Of the cool granite.
His monument never changes
Except when wet
After a day of rain.
Dark streaks
Run down over the letters,
Quite attractive.
It has been twenty-three years
Since his name was chiseled
Into that rock,
Large, deep, black block letters.
I still feel uneasy
When I visit.
I look around the yard
Searching for other caretakers
Before I speak.

I imagine
His enthusiastic reply.
I pat the stones
As I leave
And gently assure him,
"I will be back"

"Confession"

My body is seventy-two.
My desire, sixteen.
Not a sexual thing,
Performance can be humiliating.
I remember
The early days,
The early music,
The angst,
The passion,
Can't get it out of my mind.
I am
The World's Oldest Teenager.
Will I never grow up?
Maturity must be better.
I will never know.
The early times
Are emblazoned
On my brain.
I conceal these feelings
So as not to embarrass.
I remember
How I felt
About the old-timers
In my youth
People to be avoided.

Now, I am one,
So I slump in my chair,
Crank up the tunes,
Open a bottle
And pretend.

To the Young

Why am I better?
I know more than last year.
I know the fifties,
I know the sixties,
I know the seventies,
I know the eighties,
I know the nineties,
I know the two thousands,
I know the two thousand tens.
And now I am working on
The two thousand twenties.
Yes, I am better than you!

And I don't need Google
To make me look smart.

I am smart!

Sobriety Blues

I'm sittin' here
All alone
Staring at the wall
Being oh so good
With nothin' to feel
But psychic pain,
Bits and pieces
Poking at my brain.
My mind empties.
Being exemplary
Is not so cool,
Sobriety is my goal.
As my time slowly ticks
Dehydrating my soul
I make a monumental decision.
Despite all derision
I pop a cork
And watch the bubbles
Do their dance.
They like to prance
And so will I...
I pour the bottle,
Drip to dry.
A little Blues would be just right.
A little Blues relieves my plight.
I sink to euphoria.

The bubbles reign supreme.
I am invincible,
Reinforcing my guiding principle:
If it works,
Do it!

"Darkside, My Side"

Tired of the struggle?
Happiness is overrated.
I chase the euphoria.
I was elusive.
I trod another path.
I have dedicated
My life to depression.
A few suicides
And three incarcerations
In a psych ward
Earned me my degree.
I perfected my skills
By immersing
In the Blues.
I have not achieved
A masochist's expertise, yet.
Forgive the immodesty
But I am a master
Of stoicism.
Pain generates emotion;
Anger, disgust, fear,
A little paranoia.
Something to feel.
The flow
Of contented life.

Embrace it
True happiness
Achieved
By low expectations.
No medication required.

"Therapy?"

Sit down.
Put your feet up.
Relax.
It takes a while
For dreams to die.
At the least provocation
They spring back to life
Renewing the torment
Like a two-year old
Begging for candy
Just before supper.
The stress
Of unfulfilled desires
Will drag you down
Into the pit.
Squash these urges
Before they do damage.
Channel your energy
Into easy goals,
The ones that don't give you grief.
Yes, That's Right!
Lower Your Expectations!
So low
It will be an easy go.
Pop the cork.
Turn up the tunes.
Immerse yourself
In lavish praise.

Lock the door.
Shut out that Troll.
There will be no more
Of that!

"If You Are Interested?"

Getting satisfaction
Is a long sad journey. Best to stay at home,
Recede into yesteryear.
Let fantasy quell your fear.
Don't venture outside
Without a thick hide
Or you will feel
The pain of a vacuum
Encapsulating your creativity.
I know you won't listen.
Even though the tears glisten
You will keep bashing your brains
Against the wall
Of intractable superficiality.
Recycled frustration is a dangerous tool.
Stifle the desire.
And yet,
What is life
Without the drive to achieve?
Is it better to be
A formless lump of clay
Cast aside
Than to hide a crushed spirit
In a bottle of booze?
Or should we drink up
And wait for the day
When the shame goes away?

"Afterthought"

My father used to say,
"there is no shame
In failure
As long as you tried hard."

The question becomes,
"Did I try hard?"

I have no answer,
I am not through trying.

I am not dead.
My story is not over.

Is your story over?

"Simple Solution"

I wanted to be remembered
So I bought
A huge granite rock.
I had my name chiseled
In big block letters
So people could read it
From a distance.
I know how they hate
To walk in cemeteries.
Now they can greet me
As they whiz by
On the black top
On their way
To their family gatherings.
And I will give them
A nod
Showing
That I have not forgotten
To keep watch
Over their active lives.

ABOUT JAMES

Born in a tiny town in southeastern Minnesota, 1948.
Received a BA degree with an art major from Luther College,
Decorah, Iowa, 1970.
Married my high-school sweetheart.
Taught art in the public schools of Houston County, MN,
for twenty-five years.
Our only child committed suicide at age eighteen; I was
hospitalized for delusional depression three times.
Began writing poetry in my early sixties as a therapy tool.
Carved my own tombstone (and one for my wife) from a ton
of marble.
Spend my retirement writing and creating oil paintings.